Victor R. Phillips

BASIC RULES

SHORT WORDS TO LIVE BY

— Think of your cup as being half full rather than half empty.

CITI OF BOOKS

CITIOFBOOKS, INC.
3736 Eubank NE Suite A1
Albuquerque, NM 87111-3579
www.citiofbooks.com
Hotline: 1 (877) 389-2759
Fax: 1 (505) 930-7244

Ordering Information:

Quantity sales. Special discounts are available on quantity purchases by corporations, associations, and others. For details, contact the publisher at the address above.

Printed in the United States of America.

ISBN-13:   Softcover   979-8-89391-159-6

                eBook   979-8-89391-160-2

Library of Congress Control Number: 2024912024

Don't eat yellow snow.

If you see a ball rolling out into the street, slow down. There may be a kid following it.

Wear white at night.

☆

Don't step out in front of an SUV driven by a woman with kids in the back. She's on a mission.

(Flush.)

Wash your hands before eating
or rubbing your nose.

(Smile.)

If you torture statistics enough, you can make them say anything.

God teaches us patience when we
are least willing to learn it.

Grandchildren are twice a blessing; when they come and when they leave.

Pastor Don Leach

It is possible to have ten socks in your drawer with none of them matching.

When you are through saying
Something, quit talking.

(Listen.)

A short pencil is better than a short memory.

Paul Almquist

Be sure you know the punch
line before telling a joke.

Speak up. If what you are saying is important, it is important enough for everyone to hear and understand it.

There is no such thing as an illegitimate child, only illegitimate parents.

Sam Kwan

If all the people who went to sleep in church were laid end to end, they would be much more comfortable.

Pastor Don Leach

Don't spit into the wind.

If something is too good to be
true, it probably isn't true.

Some pictures are not worth a thousand words.

Plants in the garden die or go dormant in
the winter, but come to life in the spring
and yield a harvest in the summer and fall.

From the movie "Being There" with Peter Sellers

A pencil can be mightier than a sword.

A tongue can pierce like a lance.

The best way get rid of an enemy
is to make him your friend.

Abraham Lincoln

Put your eggs in several baskets.

Poor is a state of mind.

Sam Kwan

Run water slowly down your furrow so as to not wash away the good soil.

Dutch Brown, fruit rancher

The more you know, the more
you realize you don't know.

Variation on Taoism of Lao Tzu

Love is the flame of God.
Paraphrase of Song of Songs 8:6. (Darby)

Use it to purify your relationships.

It is better to bite into an apple and find a worm than to bite into an apple and find half a worm.

The early bird gets the worm, but that doesn't do much for the worm.

Some days, everything goes right. Savor those days.

Think of your cup as being half
full rather than half empty.

Your battle plan is good until the first shot.

General George Patton

Anytime you think a computer is smarter than you, just remember, it can only count to two.

I never met a man I didn't like.

Will Rogers

A soft answer turns away anger.

Paraphrase of Proverbs 15:1 (Darby)

There is something for everything to eat and something to eat everything.

Wayne Brock, tree farmer

Evil prevails when good people do nothing.

Edmund Burke (paraphrase)

Don't mail an angry letter the
same day you write it.

Wield your tongue with care.

If you don't want everyone to
know about it, don't do it.

There is "a time of war and a time of peace."

Ecclesiastes 3:8. (KJV)

The wisdom is to know the time.

Those who run in circles are known as wheels.

A little light in darkness is more effective than a little light in daylight.

Measure twice, cut once.

Build your house on solid rock.

Jesus Christ

Don't take yourself too seriously.

Test: Dip your hand in a bucket of water. Pull it out. The hole you leave represents how indispensable you are.

Sandra Day O'Connor (paraphrase)

One of life's little pleasures is doing something everybody said was impossible.

It is difficult not to say, "I told you so." Please don't.

Encourage someone in a difficult venture.

(Learn to forgive.)

The implication of the fall continues to plague us to this day, even to this very moment. Sin shattered the dream God planned for His "good works." There is no way we could completely understand the Lord's dismay, but that doesn't mean we can't relate to it in some measure. I know I do.

I grew up in a little church in Louisiana under the pastorate of Rev. W. D. Reed, one of our community's most respected members. He was well-educated and traveled throughout the state, preaching the gospel of Christ. He was a tiny man, about 5' 6" tall, and could not have weighed more than 145 pounds soaking wet. But wow, could that little man preach! Rev. Reed had no problem holding an audience spellbound as he worked through a message about God's love and the dignity of all image-bearers.

On many occasions, Rev. Reed would hit a high note in his sermons by bellowing these words, "You are somebody!" It never failed that the little church would erupt with emotion when he did. For a moment, picture this scene in your mind: Directly to the left of where Rev. Reed stood in the pulpit, on the front pew, was what we called the Mother's Bench. That's where the older ladies of the congregation sat, all dignified in their white hats and white Sunday "go-to-meeting" dresses. When Rev. Reed let loose with, "You

are somebody," get out of the way because that bench was about to get moving. Things would get hot for the next few minutes or so. Hats would fly off, and shouts of joy could be heard all the way down the street.

Likewise, to Rev. Reed's right sat the deacons dressed in Sunday suits complete with ties. They would jump to their feet, spouting words like, "Go ahead, Preacher!!!"

As a little boy, witnessing all this raw emotion was a bit scary at first. But as the years passed by, I became less perplexed and more curious. What was all this commotion about? Why would those simple words, "You are somebody," have such a significant impact on these people? After all, these were folks who meant everything in life to me. They were the people I most respected. These people loved me. They fed me. They made sure I was safe and cared for. They were the most beautiful people I knew.

It didn't matter to me that they cleaned other people's toilets, washed other people's clothes, cooked other people's food, or seemed to always have worries on their minds. These were my folks, and my greatest dream was to grow up to be just like them. Of course, they were somebody. What in the world was Rev. Reed hollering about?

As I grew older and, by God's grace, wiser, it became evident how important it was for my

people to be reminded, every now and then, that they were *somebody*. They lived in a world where, far too many times, they were treated like anything but a child of God. When they took one step forward, something ungodly would happen to drive them three steps back. After all their hard work and labor, they would have to face the reality that someone had changed the rules of the game to work against them. Far too many times, they were told, "Well, that's good enough for you people."

In a world that relegated them to second-class status, they needed a place where they could soothe their battered souls. They needed somebody to tell them, "You are somebody!" When that reality dawned on me, I began to understand and rejoice with them. After all, those little old ladies couldn't have all the fun!

But let me tell you something else that became more profound as I grew into manhood. As I started to get to know the Lord Jesus Christ, I truly began to understand the *real* meaning of "You are somebody." And that's when it became something to really shout about.

You see, *none* of us are truly *somebody* until we know Jesus as Lord and Savior. You can gain all the world has to offer, but if you don't know Jesus Christ, you are truly *not somebody*. That is one of the realities of a

shattered dream. In the shattered dream, it is *people who* determine what gives a person value. Your value might depend on how you look—straight hair versus kinky hair. Or perhaps it's how you talk—proper English or Rap. Or your value could be determined by how much money you make—if you are salaried or paid by the hour. Or maybe it has to do with which side of the tracks you live on, whom you voted for president, or if you graduated from Princeton or the school of hard knocks.

People who "are somebody" in the shattered dream world know how to disrespect the image of God that all people share. The "Shattered Dream Somebodies" are bigoted, biased, prejudiced people who don't get it. It must genuinely grieve God's heart when the "Shattered Dream Somebodies" call themselves Christian. My brothers and sisters in Christ, these ways of thinking must be challenged.

You are somebody because you have been bought with a price and are no longer your own. You are somebody because you understand that, in God's eyes, there are no second-class citizens. You are somebody because you know that God didn't choose you because you were better than anyone else. No, a loving God sovereignly chose you, and now you recognize that while you were yet a sinner,

Christ died for you (Romans 5:8). Because He died, the shattered dream takes on a different reality because we are now part of the *restored image*. You are somebody, and because you are, your heart-felt desire is that everyone else is treated like somebody, too.

Remember that you are made in the image of God, along with everyone else, because *God declares it so*. None of us had anything to do with that fact. So, we must learn to respect that *all* people are made in God's image, even in a world where we must deal with the reality of *a shattered dream*.

A SACRIFICIAL DREAM

The reality is far too many people behave as if the majority of the world's population is *not* made in the image of God. So, as we reflect on a shattered dream, we must ask, "How do we begin to change that reality? How do we bring respect to the image of God that is in all people?" When we can do this, we begin to dream God's dream.

In Peter's dream, we read the following:

> *13 And there came a voice to him: "Rise, Peter; kill and eat."14 But Peter said, "By no means, Lord; for I have never eaten anything that is common or*

*unclean." **15** And the voice came to him again a second time, "What God has made clean, do not call common." **16** This happened three times, and the thing was taken up at once to heaven.*
(Acts 10:13-16)

Perhaps we can understand Peter's dilemma. Peter was raised to follow a strict dietary regimen all his life. There were certain things he would not eat, no matter what. But even more restrictive than simple dietary issues, his culture had created a wall of separation that extended to people. That is the focus of this passage of scripture and the issue God was working to change in Peter's heart. Living by a strict code of ethics regarding what we eat is one thing, but extending this way of thinking to exclude some people is an entirely different issue.

If we allow anything to come into our mindset that prevents us from reaching out to *all* people, people who are made in the image of God, people with whom to share the gospel of Jesus Christ, we are sinning. Furthermore, if we think it's okay to share the gospel with them but then deny them full citizenship, with all its rights and privileges, both in the kingdom to come and here on earth, that is also sinning.

In Peter's dream, he had to "kill" to participate. He had to sacrifice much of what

Everybody has a life story.

Buy a homeless person a meal.

he held dear in order to please God. Peter needed to sacrifice long-held practices and beliefs to move from *disrespecting* the image of God to *embracing* it in all people. Peter had to "kill" the lie firmly rooted from how he was raised. Perhaps there are some reading these words who need to learn from his example.

To fully embrace *all* people as God's image bearers, we need to sacrifice the thinking we have been raised with and open our hearts to a new reality. This may not be an easy sacrifice, but it is necessary.

Is there anything you are holding onto that's more important than seeing others as worthy of being God's image bearers? Is there a tradition more sacred to you than removing any barrier that may prevent you from being an effective witness for Christ? Are you willing to do as Apostle Paul did when he declared that he would be willing to become all things to all men so that he may save a few? (1 Corinthians 9:22) If giving up wearing red would help you more effectively witness to someone concerning the love of Jesus Christ, would you be willing to give up red?

Beloved, these are the issues we need to grapple with as we seek to serve God as our highest privilege. There is nothing more critical any of us could do than to see a poor soul saved from an eternity in hell, separated from the love of God. Are you willing to "kill"

and sacrifice anything you hold dear for the sake of Christ? Are you willing to participate in the shared dream? Would you make yourself available to dream God's dream?

We are all familiar with Jesus' many teachings about what should be paramount in our lives. In Mark 8:36, Jesus said:

> *For what does it profit a man to gain the whole world and forfeit his soul?*

Let me ask you, "For what does it cost a man if he gains Christ and forfeits all of the profit the world has to offer?"

If we are genuinely on board with the supremacy of gaining Christ in our lives, what does it matter if we never gain anything that the world holds dear? What if we truly lived as if we fully embraced becoming all things for all people so that we may save some? How could we continue to hold on to earthly pride and standards while image-bearers of God suffer and are killed and oppressed all over the world? And we must never forget the people in our own backyards.

Our hearts should grieve for all of humanity—the image bearers of God— suffering from injustice. We should grieve in our own country when our leaders promote any barrier dividing us by race, ethnicity, or any other man-made barrier. God declared we

all are His image bearers, even after the fall. Believers and unbelievers alike, we need to respect all people as bearers of God's image. We must learn to sacrifice any dream that is not God's dream.

A SHARED DREAM

"**D**reaming *God's* Dream" means the dream is not our own creation but a dream God shares with us. And it is only through Christ that we can dream God's dream. It is God's dream that representatives from all the people of the earth come to embrace the gospel of Jesus Christ and join with Him for all eternity. God is extending this invitation to everyone. Taste and see that the Lord is good (Psalm 34:8). That invitation must go out to everyone. That is God's dream.

We must never let our personal bias, based on experience or a distorted worldview, stand in the way of sharing God's dream. We must fully embrace everyone that God draws to Himself to join in the banquet of the Lord.

Jesus presents an exciting dream for us in Luke 12. It is a dream of inclusion, where those of privilege have rejected God's vision.

So the servant came and reported these things to his master. Then the master of the house

*became angry and said to his servant, 'Go out
quickly to the streets and lanes of the city, and
bring in the poor and crippled and blind and
lame.' And the servant said, 'Sir, what you
commanded has been done, and still there is
room.' And the master said to the servant, 'Go
out to the highways and hedges and compel
people to come in, that my house may be
filled. For I tell you, none of those men who
were invited shall taste my banquet.'"*
(Luke 12:21-24)

As children of God, we are privileged to be
invited to the banquet of God. In this parable,
guests of the King placed their own agenda
ahead of the King's agenda. They had
their *own* priorities driving their agenda.
There was no room for them to mingle with
the "common folk" around town. In their
minds, they were better than everyone else.
But the King wasn't about to let their narrow-
mindedness stand in the way of *His* agenda.

There is a world full of His image bearers
who, if invited, are ready to join in on the
feast. He has room in His kingdom for every
one of them. That is a dream God dreams. And
it's a dream He wants all believers to share
with Him. Could you share that dream? A
banquet is happening, and God wants the
"nobodies" out there to come to Him because
God and fellow believers see them as
"somebody."

If an authentic, born-again believer in Jesus Christ walked into your life right now, would they be overwhelmed with the presence of God in your life? It is my dream that no man-made barrier prevents them from joining the body of Christ if God were moving them in that direction.

If you find yourself reading these words and do not know the Lord, my dream would be that you become so drawn to His Word and that you be prompted by a desire to connect with authentic Christians reflecting a loving, welcoming image of God to all people.

Remember, God's dream isn't about quotas —so many of "this type" or so many of "that type." If we follow that line of thinking, we will miss the boat. God's dream is to eliminate all man-made barriers that could stop people from joining with God at His table, a table filled with fellow believers who value the worthiness of *all* God's image bearers. And if God decrees that the guests at His table will be 100% green or 100% purple or 100% blue people, then that would be all right with me if that's the dream God dreams for our Church.

If we can look out at Christ's Church and see the same vision the Apostle John saw in Rev. 7:9, we would be blessed indeed.

"After this I looked, and behold, a great multitude that no one could number, from

every nation, from all tribes and peoples and
languages, standing before the throne and
before the Lamb, clothed in white robes, with
palm branches in their hands..."
(Revelation 7:9)

Let this be a call to all believers to dream God's dream, to go out into the highways and byways, respecting that *all* men are created equal in God's sight and that all image-bearers are welcomed in the house of the Lord! Will you join us?

CONCLUSION

Perhaps you or a loved one has deeply embedded memories of not being treated as an image bearer of God. These difficult experiences do not need to hinder us one little bit because we know, without a doubt, that we are somebody because of the man, Jesus Christ. God's Word clearly states that every human being has been made in His image, and we can stand on that truth.

As we have worked through these scriptures, I'm sure you've recognized a common theme of eating and banquets.

- Adam and Eve undoubtedly enjoyed an unequal feast in the Garden of Eden.

- Peter's vision was full of food and eating.

- Jesus taught about inviting people to come and enjoy His banquet.

- John in Revelation described the banquet feast that will take place in heaven.

This idea of breaking bread together is important to God.

My wife's father, Lewis Curtis, is a man I deeply respect. Born in 1927, he was forced to endure some very dark times over his 90 years of life due to inexcusable, reprehensible racism. I asked Mr. Curtis what a man could do to demonstrate to him that he was viewed as an equal image bearer of God. My father-in-law answered that if a man invited him home to eat with him, that would represent a solid first step in communicating that he was viewed as an equal by that man. I think that is significant.

Maybe you can think of someone of a different race, culture, or background that you could invite over for a meal, with the sole purpose of acknowledging and honoring them as an image bearer of God. I agree with my wife's father. I think that breaking bread with someone different from you would begin to make a difference in this shattered world.

We are to respect *all* of God's image bearers. If we do, it is only with God's grace that we can begin to dream God's dream, a dream that, unlike the popular song we've heard so often, is indeed possible.

PRAYER

Father, Your glory is on display in Your creation. The heavenly host declares Your glory. The earth declares Your glory. And in Your crowning act of creation, humanity, as Your image bearer, was charged with bringing You the highest degree of glory. But through a single act of selfishness, the dream was shattered. That life-changing choice replaced the dream with a horrifying nightmare, highlighting the evil in our midst. Yet all was not lost. You had a plan to revive the dream. You sacrificed Your Son so the dream of restoration with You and each other would be restored. So let us once again dream Your dream, and in doing so, your glory will be on display throughout all of Your creation! Amen.

ABOUT CLIMBING ANGEL PUBLISHING

Climbing Angel Publishing exists for the purpose of sharing stories of hope and encouragement, aiding in the gathering together of community, and supporting the process of betterment. The following books are available at ClimbingAngel.com and major bookstores.

ADULT BOOKS: (Romans 8:28-30)

In His Image by Sam Polson
(English, Romanian, & Mandarin)
By Faith by Sam Polson (English & Romanian)
My Birthday Gift to Jesus by Lisa Soland
Without Ceasing by Dr. Dennis Davidson
SonLight: Daily Light from the Pages of God's Word
by Sam Polson
Corona Victus: Conquering the Virus of Fear
by Sam Polson (English & Romanian)
Art Bushing: His Diary, Letters, & Photographs of WWII
by Art Bushing
Art & Dotty: His Diary, Their Letters & Photographs of WWII by Art Bushing
Trimisul by Stan Johnson (Romanian)
Life Changing Prayer by Sam Polson
The Climbing Angel Christmas Treasury,
variety of authors
J. Calvin Coolidge: Letters from the Korean War
by J. Calvin Coolidge
Stories from Kingman, AZ: The Heart of Historic Route 66
by Loren B. Wilson
Pathways: Ancient Paths from the Pages of the Old Testament by Sam Polson

THE SINGLE SERMON SERIES: (1 Peter 3:15)

Jesus is Alive! by Mike Sager
My Mother's Bible by Sam Polson
The Lost Boys by Jake Bishop
Melchizedek: A Shadow of Christ by Jerry Scheumann
A Servant of Christ by James Alan Lynch
Dreaming God's Dream by Dr. Al Cage

CHILDREN'S BOOKS: (Philippians 4:8)

The Christmas Tree Angel by Lisa Soland
The Unmade Moose by Lisa Soland
Thump by Lisa Soland
Somebunny To Love by Lisa Soland
(English & Mandarin)
The Truth About God's Rainbow by Lisa Soland
God's Promises by Lisa Soland
The Boy & The Bagel Necklace by Lisa Soland
God's Hands and Feet by Lisa Soland
I Like To Be Quiet by Joni Caldwell
Wheels Off! by Karlie Saumier
Ella's Trip of a Lifetime by Melanie Ewbank
Because You Are Mine by Gayle Childress Greene
Jeremy Plays the Blues by Amy Oden Simpson
Bad Hair Day by Jasmyne Simpkins
I Like To Read by Joni Caldwell
Trunks Up! by Karlie Saumier
Perusha's Paradise by Bette Reed Smith
Ruby and the Treasure Within
by Tonya Celeste Hobbs
Abby, the Wonder Dog & her Warrior Princess
by Melanie Ewbank
The Christmas Coat by Lisa Soland
Danger Around the Bend by Karlie Saumier

If you take thirty minutes to figure out how to do an hour's job in thirty minutes, you've saved thirty minutes.

Oscar Rash

Take a horse to water. You can't make him drink, but he may think about it.

(Don't expect life to be fair.)

Give credit when credit is due.

If what you are doing is right, do it boldly.

Put your mind in gear before engaging your mouth.

Perform acts of kindness.

Serve a meal at the mission.

Recycle.

Say, "Thank you."

Be like a duck, cool and calm on the surface but paddling swiftly underneath.

If you find a nail in the street, pick it up.

Don't multitask while driving.

Give workers a fair wage.

$

An eye for an eye makes the whole
world blind.

Mahatma Gandhi

Actions speak louder than words.

Don't stop to chat in the middle of foot traffic. Move to the side.

Return shopping carts.

*another nation, but God has shown me that I
should not call any person common or
unclean.*

A SHATTERED DREAM

As a direct consequence of the fall of Adam
and Eve, God's dream that we all would
respect every individual as a bearer of God's
image was destroyed. Adam and Eve had no
idea of the cosmic implications their single act
of disobedience would have on all of God's
creation. But, in one selfish move, the dream
of eternal fellowship with God was shattered.
God conveyed his dismay by asking Eve a
question.

*Then the Lord God said to the woman,
"What is this that you have done?"*
(Genesis 3:13)

That question, "What is this that you have
done?" must have caused both Adam and Eve
to fall back in shame and fear. The
disappointment in God's voice must have
driven them to fear for their very existence.
Can you imagine the God of creation speaking
these words to you in response to your
sin? *"What have you done?"*

In verse 4, Cornelius responds to the Lord in fear.

> *And he stared at him in terror and said,*
> *"What is it, Lord?" And he said to him, "Your*
> *prayers and your alms have ascended as a*
> *memorial before God.*

Overcoming his fear, Cornelius responds to the Lord in obedience.

Meanwhile, Peter, Jewish, a born-again believer in Jesus Christ, called to the office of Apostle, a pillar of the Church, is also dreaming God's dream. Peter is confronted with some beliefs inconsistent with God's dream. He awakes from God's dream, understanding that certain things must change. God brings Cornelius and Peter together so that the two men may participate as co-equals in God's dream.

Cornelius and Peter went on to meet, and that is where we pick up the story beginning in Acts 10:25-28.

> **25** *When Peter entered, Cornelius met him*
> *and fell down at his feet and worshiped*
> *him.* **26** *But Peter lifted him up, saying,*
> *"Stand up; I too am a man."* **27** *And as he*
> *talked with him, he went in and found many*
> *persons gathered.* **28** *And he said to them,*
> *"You yourselves know how unlawful it is for*
> *a Jew to associate with or to visit anyone of*

If you see someone spill something, don't just laugh and move on; help them clean it up.

Don't say "hi" to your friend Jack in an airport.

The Walla Walla way is cooperation.

Don't lick dry ice or metal in freezing weather.

Walk with a knife pointed down.

Don't startle a sleeping dog.

Talk before you sue.

Pen and paper can cut.

Hatred ceases by love.

Gautama Buddha

Most people's attention span is inversely proportional to the wrinkles in their bladder.

17 Now while Peter was inwardly perplexed as to what the vision that he had seen might mean, behold, the men who were sent by Cornelius, having made inquiry for Simon's house, stood at the gate 18 and called out to ask whether Simon who was called Peter was lodging there. 19 And while Peter was pondering the vision, the Spirit said to him, "Behold, three men are looking for you. 20 Rise and go down and accompany them without hesitation, for I have sent them." 21 And Peter went down to the men and said, "I am the one you are looking for. What is the reason for your coming?" 22 And they said, "Cornelius, a centurion, an upright and God-fearing man, who is well spoken of by the whole Jewish nation, was directed by a holy angel to send for you to come to his house and to hear what you have to say." 23 So he invited them in to be his guests.

The next day he rose and went away with them, and some of the brothers from Joppa accompanied him. 24 And on the following day they entered Caesarea. Cornelius was expecting them and had called together his relatives and close friends.

This story in Acts is about a vision or dream given by God to a Gentile and a Jew. The Gentile, Cornelius, is a God-fearer devoted to serving God. God honors Cornelius by giving him a vision that would really shake him up.

God come in and say to him, "Cornelius."
4 And he stared at him in terror and said, "What is it, Lord?" And he said to him, "Your prayers and your alms have ascended as a memorial before God. **5** And now send men to Joppa and bring one Simon who is called Peter. **6** He is lodging with one Simon, a tanner, whose house is by the sea." **7** When the angel who spoke to him had departed, he called two of his servants and a devout soldier from among those who attended him, **8** and having related everything to them, he sent them to Joppa.

9 The next day, as they were on their journey and approaching the city, Peter went up on the housetop about the sixth hour to pray. **10** And he became hungry and wanted something to eat, but while they were preparing it, he fell into a trance **11** and saw the heavens opened and something like a great sheet descending, being let down by its four corners upon the earth. **12** In it were all kinds of animals and reptiles and birds of the air. **13** And there came a voice to him: "Rise, Peter; kill and eat." **14** But Peter said, "By no means, Lord; for I have never eaten anything that is common or unclean." **15** And the voice came to him again a second time, "What God has made clean, do not call common." **16** This happened three times, and the thing was taken up at once to heaven.

The worst way to find a lost needle
is to pick it up in your foot.

When setting up a buffet, place the utensils and napkins at the end of the food line.

Dogs don't bark at parked cars.

Lynne Cheney

Only after you attain perfection should you pass judgment on others.

(When someone offers you a Tic-Tac, take it.)

Read instructions.

Marry a person you love to talk to.

Don't believe all you hear, spend all
you have, or sleep all you want.

When you say, "I love you." mean it.

When you say, "I'm sorry," look the person in the eye.

out with a mighty hand and redeemed you
from the house of slavery, from the hand of
Pharaoh king of Egypt."

Israel lost sight of this proclamation and became puffed up over the blessings God bestowed on them. They thought they were special, and because of this, they would lose a healthy respect for all human beings as made in the image of God.

We all know the old saying that to the victor goes the spoils. Unfortunately, those in positions of power and privilege are prone to adopt the mantle that God has given them a special dispensation of His image. That is simply not the case. Those who claim Jesus Christ as Lord and Savior must especially be challenged to resist this thinking. Our Lord demands that we respect *all people* as image bearers of God.

People have intrinsic worth. God-given worth is the central issue throughout the scripture we are studying in this book. Let's begin by reviewing Acts 10:1-28.

1 At Caesarea there was a man named
Cornelius, a centurion of what was known as
the Italian Cohort, 2 a devout man who
feared God with all his household, gave alms
generously to the people, and prayed
continually to God. 3 About the ninth hour of
the day he saw clearly in a vision an angel of

As believers, we are equipped to see every human being with new eyes. We can see our fellow man with eyes that have been opened to the reality of how precious people are in God's sight. After all, scripture tells us that God "desires all people to be saved and to come to the knowledge of the truth" (1 Timothy 2:4), therefore becoming image bearers.

And image bearers are just that—image bearers. There are no *big* image bearers versus *small* image bearers. There are no *wide* image bearers versus *thin* image bearers and no *first-class* image bearers versus *second-class* image bearers. We are all created to bear God's image.

God has always stood by this paradigm. Even in choosing the nation of Israel as His "special instrument," God made it clear that it was not because they were *better* than any other people on earth. This fact is made clear for us in Deuteronomy 7:6-8.

"For you are a people holy to the Lord your God. The Lord your God has chosen you to be a people for his treasured possession, out of all the peoples who are on the face of the earth. It was not because you were more in number than any other people that the Lord set his love on you and chose you, for you were the fewest of all peoples, but it is because the Lord loves you and is keeping the oath that he swore to your fathers, that the Lord has brought you

Be engaged at least six months
before you marry.

Never laugh at anyone's dreams.
Dreams made the United States.

Don't judge people by their relatives.

Think quickly, talk slowly.

Great love and great achievements
involve great risk.

(When you lose, you win a lesson.)

> *"Whoever sheds the blood of man, by man
> shall his blood be shed, for God made man in
> his own image."*
> (Genesis 9:6)

This truth is presented after the fall and represents a significant doctrinal issue. Through God's decree and action, all people are His image bearers. Ironically, sin gets in the way of understanding and accepting this fundamental truth from God—that all men are created in His image. This fact has nothing to do with one's religious status, nationality, economic status, sexual orientation, or political party. All men are God's image bearers. Flawed as all of us are, we still carry in our very being the privileged status of being created in the image of God.

THE SECOND ADAM

Jesus Christ, the second Adam, was also the bearer of God's image, but unlike the first Adam, he was the *perfect* image bearer. Through His perfect life, Jesus provides His followers the opportunity to renew what was impacted by Adam's sin. Through sanctification, we can begin the process of restoring our status as God's image bearers on earth.

THE FIRST ADAM

I am sure you are as encouraged as I am to know that despite the desperate predicament created by Adam's transgression of God's explicit command, all is not lost. God had a plan of restoration for us already worked out ahead of time.

The first Adam, perfect as God's image bearer, lost this status when he sinned. The doctrine of original sin presents the reality that when Adam sinned as the representative of all members of the human race, we all inherited his sinful nature. The Bible states in Romans 3:23:

> *"...for all have sinned and fallen short of the glory of God..."*

Each of us has inherited from Adam a sinful nature that corrupts our personhood and our ability to reflect the image of God properly. Adam's sin resulted in the image becoming distorted but not totally lost.

After the fall, the Bible continues to teach that man is made in God's image, and that gives value to *all* people.

Remember the three R's: respect for self; respect for others, and responsibility for all your actions.

Don't let a little dispute ruin a great friendship.

(Correct mistakes immediately.)

Smile when phoning or talking to a blind person. They will hear it in your voice.

☺

Spend some time quietly alone.

A true friend is one who reaches for
your hand and touches your heart.

♥

Always check your spell check.

Don't assume anything.

Save your work on your computer often.

Doctors should not say, "Oops," or "I've never done that before," in earshot of a patient.

If you wait long enough a new study will come out that will justify your way of life.

NBC News

Don't bloviate.

Bill O'Reilly

In case of a sudden drop in air pressure secure your own mask before helping others.

Airline stewardesses

Dedication...

I grew up in southern Louisiana while the devastating effects of the Jim Crow South were being addressed through the Civil Rights Movement. During that time, my family attended a little church on the banks of the False River in Pointe Coupee Parish. There, Zion Traveler Baptist Church members helped nourish in me an unyielding desire to honor God by dreaming big even when facing the greatest opposition. Dreaming God's Dream is dedicated to their legacy and the inspiration I gained from that little congregation, who, despite the odds stacked against them, worked relentlessly for the advancement of all people.

– Dr. Al Cage

Dreaming God's Dream
Written by Dr. Al Cage

Edited by Lisa Soland
Text copyright © 2024 Dr. Al Cage

Most Scripture quotations are from the ESV® Bible (The Holy Bible, English Standard Version®), copyright © 2001 by Crossway, a publishing ministry of Good News Publishers. Used by permission. All rights reserved.

Published in 2024 by:
Climbing Angel Publishing
PO Box 32381
Knoxville, Tennessee 37930
http://www.ClimbingAngel.com

First Edition: March 2024
Printed in the United States of America

Graphic Design: Climbing Angel Publishing

ISBN: 978-1-956218-31-2
Library of Congress Control Number: 2024902892

Dreaming GOD'S Dream

by Dr. Al Cage

Publishing
Angel
Climbing

6

The Single Sermon Series

Dreaming
GOD'S Dream